THE THINGS WE SEE : **HOUSES**

by LIONEL BRETT, M.A., A.R.I.B.A.

D1513697

PENGUIN BOOKS, WEST DRAYTON, MIDDLESEX 1947

To CLOUGH WILLIAMS ELLIS

*

ACKNOWLEDGEMENTS

I wish to thank the Conway Librarian of the National Buildings Record, the Housing Centre and the *Architectural Review* for their help with illustrations, and all those architects who have lent photographs of their work, especially Messrs. Wells Coates and Patrick Gwynne, E. Goldfinger, Oliver Hill, Denys Lasdun, B. Lubetkin, Miss Sadie Speight and Professor Basil Ward.
Acknowledgements are also due to the Council of Industrial Design for general assistance in the preparation of this and other volumes in the series.

THE ILLUSTRATIONS

The numbers against the illustrations refer to the captions printed in italics on the same or the facing pages, and also to the details of architects, copyright-holders, etc., given on page 64.
The drawings are by Alfredo Martinez Alonso, with the exception of those on pages 7, 18, 47, 55, 57 and 58, which are by the author.

NOTE TO THE READER

THIS book contains a collection of photographs of modern English houses, some good, some decent, some frankly bad. The latter, unfortunately, make up far too great a proportion of *The Things We See*. The author, in his choice of illustrations and his text, attempts, like the other writers in this series, to make us critically aware of our surroundings. Study the illustrations carefully, therefore, and then make your own comparisons out of doors.

MADE AND PRINTED IN GREAT BRITAIN

Houses live and die ; there is a time for building
And a time for living and generation
And a time for the wind to break the loosened pane
And to shake the wainscot where the field-mouse trots
And to shake the tattered arras woven with a silent motto.

T. S. ELIOT

EXCUSE

THE TRUTH IS that to write a book about Houses is as wild an undertaking as to write a book about People. Thinking of the great multitude of English houses, row upon row smoking into city sunsets or shyly clinging to the skirts of village elms, the mind reels. This is a private world. Behind the decent or the defiant street face, behind the lamplit curtain, a personality as varied and as subtle as the human character itself is hidden. The neat photographer stops in a silent street, focuses, waits while a few children freeze and stare ; then the sun comes out, the house smiles a meaningless public smile, and off he goes winding his film, having discovered nothing. After the builder has gone, and until death by bomb or pickaxe, the house is a home, and can only be judged by processes quite beyond the scope of this series. All through, as we discuss fashion in the house's face and form and clothing, it will do no harm to realise that we are skating the surface of a lake of unknown depth.

ERRATUM

The references in the index on page 64 to the houses illustrated on pages 42 and 43 have been inadvertently transposed. Messrs. Tayler & Green are the Architects of No. 42 ('Fred'), not of No. 43 ('Clarence').

This book, then, is about the looks of modern houses. How to turn them out in large numbers ; how to rationalise their form, standardise their components, accelerate their erection and cheapen their cost, all these technical problems have been tackled, and some to the best of our present knowledge solved, in the last few years. Anyhow, it is too late now for the consumer to do anything about it. Once the factory is tooled up and its products begin to roll off the production lines it is possible to modify design, but it is useless to have afterthoughts about the method of production. Now is the time, as the houses begin to go up, when technical questions are naturally relegated to the backroom boys and the public turns its attention to appearances. And as the years go by, and it becomes possible, instead of being issued with a utility house, to go out and have one made to measure, the looks of houses will begin to matter more than ever.

It is debatable whether the use of one's eyes in a modern English city is, on balance, a source of pleasure or of pain. The argument is similar to another which has become popular in the twentieth century : whether the cow is a happier creature than the human being. In both cases no firm answer can be given because we have no experience of one of the alternatives. It is, in fact, impossible not to use one's eyes. Take the four houses on the opposite page. Which do you like best ? In making your decision, I doubt whether you are concerned with construction, arrangement or economy. You make an æsthetic choice, just as when you choose a tie or a wallpaper. If you regret the choice, you can give the former away and distemper the latter, but if you choose bad architecture, posterity will have to suffer for it just as we now endure the too substantial edifices of our Victorian ancestors. It is important therefore to choose well. We cannot fairly blame the builder, whose object, after all, is not to educate his customers, but to sell his houses.

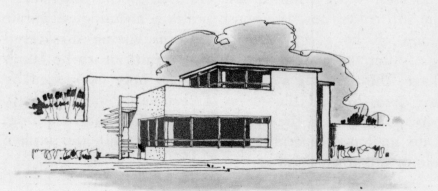

1

1815

2

1885

3

1925

4

1938

THE RETURN OF THE PRODIGAL SON

To choose well one must be able to say, not merely, " I like this ", but " This is good ". To acquire that much certainty, and all the fun and enjoyment that go with it, one needs a little knowledge. Just as in judging a car one ought to look under the bonnet, so in judging a house one should know something of the designer's problems and alternatives. So in this little book we go behind the scenes with the modern architect and watch his struggle to breathe life into the bare bones of site, plan and structure.

This post-war architect, unless he is very eccentric, begins where his predecessor left off. In other words, his foundation is the style and technique that were called " modern " in the thirties. Callow and immature though it is, this kind of architecture is too deeply rooted in the soil of our time to be pushed over. Direct and candid, delighting in the mechanical and contemptuous of the artificial, it reflects us as neatly as the Jeep and the Spitfire. Its pedigree, which there is no need to recapitulate, is simple and respectable. Art and science being where they were by 1900, it was bound to happen. " Damp, cracked and leaky ' architecture ' ", as Lethaby was writing in 1911, " must give way to buildings as efficient as a bicycle"— a thing which has since proved to be easier said than done.

Of course, your contemporary architect, divided from his predecessors by a war and heaven knows what mental upheavals, is no more likely to rest content with the modernism of the thirties than was Lethaby with the stylism of the nineties. But, inescapably, that is where he starts, and if we are to understand him, we must start there too.

Before the War, this modern architecture was a minority movement, suffering its share of abuse, jokes, misunderstanding and phoney reproduction. But yesterday's minority is tomorrow's majority. The pioneer experiments of the 'thirties will become the general practice of the 'fifties. And that is this little book's excuse. It will attempt, within its limits, to revaluate the domestic work of the 'thirties, that haunted decade in which the modern house appeared in England, briefly flourished, and went down before the blackout ; and to pick out therefrom whatever is of value to us builders of today. It will exclude flats, shacks, maisonettes and mansions. Lastly, it is written not for the architect, but for the man and woman who pay the piper, and have every right to call the tune.

It would seem that the tree is an element essential to our comfort, and its presence in the city is a sort of caress, a kindly thing in the midst of our severe creations.

LE CORBUSIER

SETTING

JUST AS A person is conditioned by heredity and environment, so a house is conditioned by its setting. Neither is intelligible in isolation. Broadly, there are three kinds of setting, the street, the plot and the country. The house in the street (and here we include squares, greens, terraces and crescents) is like the soldier in the platoon. His face is his own but he wears uniform and stands at attention, dressed by the right, facing front. So the terrace house has its own face (its yellow door, its geraniums, its muslin curtains) but accepts the discipline of the larger group. This tension between community and individuality may fortify a strong character and ruin a weak one.

1

3

THE

TERRACE

HOUSE

5

2

HEYDAY

4

COLLAPSE

6

REVIVAL

9

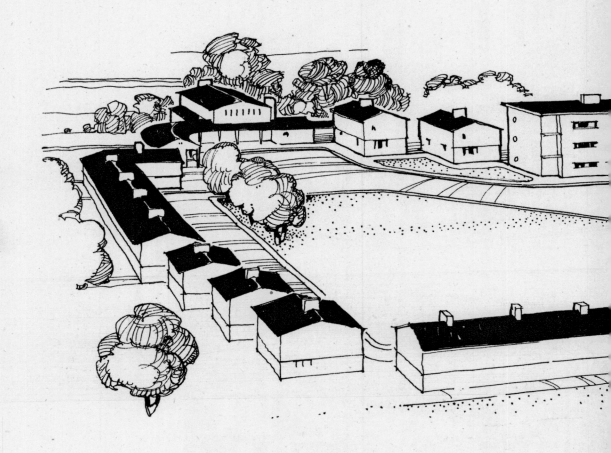

The house on the plot reclines at ease, like the man eating his lunch in the park, not alone but introspective. It is an anomalous situation. There is neither the willing submission of the town house nor the complete freedom of the country house to put itself where it likes, even to remodel its view where it is rich enough to possess it. Conflicting motives occur. The sun may be on one side, the view on another, the road on a third. Local customs and materials may suggest themselves, trees and other existing features need consideration. It is easy, of course, (or it was) to ignore all these problems, wipe the site clean, squeeze into it the maximum legal number of semi-detached " homes ", doll them up with cheap ornament and sell the lot at fabulous profit to people desperate for a roof over their

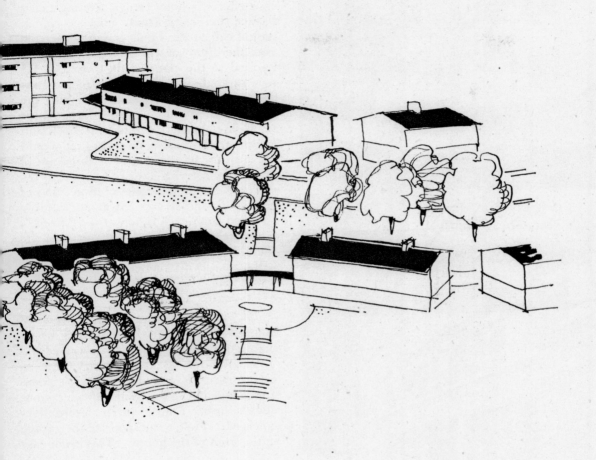

heads. Let us, however, imagine a crowded estate, but an honest effort to do the best for all. Here are three sample problems that crop up at once.

1. *Orientations*.

It would be pleasant if all living rooms faced south-west, but if all houses are to face the same way we must double the number of access roads and raise rents or selling prices accordingly. Is it worth it? Moreover, houses built in parallel rows are less pleasant to live among than houses grouped about squares and crescents or facing each other across friendly greens.

There is a compromise solution. If every house has a through living room running from front to back, it can face any direction and the sun will get in.

2. *Front versus Back.*

It would be pleasant if living rooms covered the whole garden frontage of a terrace house, so that gardens, which should call to mind daisies and deckchairs and the hum of bees, need no longer resound to the clang of dustbins and the roar of coal-sacks. But that means putting kitchen, dustbin, coalhole and the rest at the " front ". The " front " (or street-side) in fact becomes the back and our main entrance is, as perhaps it should be, " up the garden path ". But what of the visitor arriving by car ?

There is a compromise solution : to put both main and service entrances, suitably screened from each other, at the " front ". Ultimately, with the development of the roundsman's hatch, the service entrance will probably disappear altogether.

3. *Garages.*

The garage, without which soon no house will be complete, constitutes a new planning problem which has received too little attention in this country. In its early stages it was treated as a mere appendage in the way that new inventions always are. Later, three alternatives emerged. First, to incorporate the garage in the front of the house. This is not easy

1 & 2. *Main and service entrances and garage neatly contrived in the same elevation. There is no solution to this problem by " traditional " design methods. The little Georgian front door just cannot take it.*

to do well.   There is a danger of the huge maw of the garage distracting attention from the front door.   Second, to build garages in pairs between pairs of houses, forming a not unsatisfactory linkage between blocks.   This solves the æsthetic problem in an easy way and is almost bound to look decent.   Third, in urban development, to make use of odd corners of the site to build garages in blocks at an easy distance from the blocks of houses they serve.   This is economical in frontage, but obviously less convenient than the other methods, where direct access from house to garage is possible.   Needless to say, any one of these three solutions can be handled well, and can be handled badly.

But the trickiest problem of all raised by the modern narrow plot is the relationship of the individual house to its neighbours.   That peculiarly English compromise, the semi-detached house, is open to two serious objections.   First, it is wasteful of ground.   Those five-yard draughty spaces between pairs could accommodate almost as many extra houses, and the space saved could go to more generous private or public gardens, or alternatively, could lower the price of every house.   Secondly, the continual

3

4

5

3. Islington, 1820. Ingenious solution of the problem of building a terrace on a slope.

4. Environs of almost any provincial railway station, 1880. The street, as centre of life and fun, survives.

5. Any Council estate, 1930. The street has become a suburban road, and life withdrawn to the back garden.

THE FLIGHT FROM THE STREET

" That chicken-farm feeling."

repetition of small oblong buildings produces a restless and boxy skyline and gives the resident that chicken-farm feeling that is an element in suburban discontent. Hence the growing movement to return to the friendly terrace, square and crescent of our Georgian tradition, with all their advantages in economy, cosiness and communal facilities. It will be interesting to see whether the Englishman's neighbourliness triumphs over his independence, or whether, as is more likely, the game is drawn.

Where the plot is larger and neighbours can be planted out and ignored, our modern house may enjoy within modest limits the happy self-determination of the country-house. It is then that the modern architect comes forward with proposals for a new way of living. Until science freed building from the tyranny of the weight-bearing wall, people thought of the house as a solid oblong box with a door through which one could reach a carefully-planned and neatly-pruned garden.

House and garden were separate objects; in summer the garden bright and green, the house cool and shuttered, in winter the garden dank and dark, the house cosy and introspective. Only in the Victorian conservatory was some attempt made to enjoy nature indoors, and there the interest was botanical rather than æsthetic. Then, at roughly the same moment, came plate glass, central heating, frame construction, the discovery of sunlight and sky and a new delight in the natural profusion of trees and plants. All now needed was a designer to effect the necessary synthesis and in due course (it was around 1900) he appeared. The result was sensational. The garden invaded the house, the house invaded the garden. One could no longer say where one ended and the other began. Shielded by a tough invisible wall of glass, which in summer slides away, it becomes possible to take part in the sparrow's existence or watch the wide procession of clouds across the western horizon.

Sniggers are audible at this point, and the usual references to the English climate. The answer is that if you do not wish to buy, there is no obligation. But in compiling a profit-and-loss statement on the modern house, it is only fair to set to its credit the friendly relationship it has established with sun, trees and plants.

It would be dishonest not to add that this treaty with Nature had its advantages for the modern architect. Her summer foliage does a great deal to hide the nakedness of his buildings ; her elegant winter tracery to soften their angularity. Denied by the circumstances of his time a natural ability to create ornament himself, the architect accepted with a sigh of relief Nature's profuse decoration, and could often be heard claiming that his plain surfaces were specially designed to make the most of it.

At the other end of the scale is the town house, particularly the intruder into an existing street. This was a perennial bone of contention before the war. On one side were the antiquarians, the preservationists, the genuine lovers of the English tradition and the stodgier local authorities. To this faction a white wall was a red rag and a flat roof was the badge of bolshevism. Creative modern architecture and its bogus parodies fell alike under the ban.*

continued on page 18

2

3

The small house in the landscape, showing that good design is more important than the use of " local materials ". 2. 1936, 3. 1946.

---

*The trouble is that it takes a trained eye to distinguish the modern from the modernistic. With earlier styles it was easy : the genuine was old, the fake was new. In our day the two go on together and the creative Jekyll is dogged by a clumsy Hyde who picks up the more superficial aspects of the modern manner (the flat roof, the corner window, the strong horizontal) and attaches a jazzy version of them to his otherwise quite conventional buildings. The novice is advised to look for *Simplicity* and for the time being to treat *Smartness*, *Streamline* and *Luxury* with suspicion.

1

2

THE CULT OF FRESH AIR

3

4

The cry was local materials (the muddier in colour the better), hand-made tiles, small panes and thatched filling stations. In their irritation, modern architects were sometimes equally unreasonable and tried to prove, what was quite impossible, that a modern building, merely by being honestly contemporary, would fit into any company. The truth is, of course, that modern construction involves such a revolutionary scale, such unprecedented smoothness of texture, that it is fully capable (however good in itself) of making nonsense of a lovely old composition, whether formal or informal. The rule must be that where what exists is (as is usual) planless and chaotic, the designer can safely ignore it ; but where by design or accident it has a unity, he is no architect if he fails to acknowledge it—not by boring imitation, but by politeness of scale and texture. He may even, if he is brave, bring off a deliberate discord. But there we must leave him. The cloudy region of the Picturesque is no place for penguins.

" Nature's profuse decoration."

1

2

Tudorbethan

4

Neo-Georgian

3

5

VICTORIAN

ODERN

6

Neo=Victorian

does not yet exist but no doubt soon will.

7

Modernistic

1. In stone

2. In concrete

ADDITIONS AND ALTERATIONS

3. In brick

These pictures confirm that on the whole the greater the value of the old work, the more difficult it is to make a successful addition.

The age of crustacean building has given way to the age of vertebrates.

LEWIS MUMFORD

SKELETON

NOW TO COME to the house itself. Because the structure controls the plan, and the plan controls the appearance, it is impossible to discuss appearances without being aware of the skeleton behind them. Until the Industrial Revolution, there were two ways of constructing a house. The first and oldest was to erect a *frame* of pieces of wood and then to fill up the spaces or *panels* with some easily manipulable material such as mud or wattle or bricks. This method survives to this day except that for wood we can now substitute pieces of steel or reinforced concrete capable of considerably greater spans for their thickness, and that to mud, etc., we prefer a whole range of dry and handy sheeting materials from plate-glass to asbestos-cement. The second method was to construct the house out of a large number of small *units*, such as bricks, blocks of stone, pieces of wood, tiles and small bits of glass. This method, which unlike the first is called for some reason the " traditional " method of building, also survives to this day, and is one reason why so many of our houses copy old patterns ; but there is a tendency to enlarge the size of the units up to quite large sections of wall or roof. This tendency is known as prefabrication.

To these two ancient methods of building, modern technique has added a third, known among architects as *monolithic* construction. Here the whole structure is cast in one piece, as it were, of concrete reinforced by an invisible web of steel. Walls, floors and roof strengthen each other like the parts of a chest-of-drawers (the resemblance of early experiments to this prototype is unmistakable), and the more surely in that the building is completely jointless. Wide openings can be cut as easily as you cut a hole in a packing-case. We shall see in the next chapter the effects on appearances of this innovation.

These differences in the structure of a building are bound to influence its arrangement. Houses put together out of a number of identical units, as were those of the Renaissance, show a regular repetition of parts and are naturally symmetrical. Houses erected on the frame-and-panel principle, as were many of those of the Middle Ages, escape this limitation, and can freely adapt themselves to convenience or fancy. So that the reappearance (in its new form) of frame and panel construction would have been likely anyhow to induce a general loosening-up of the Victorian plan.

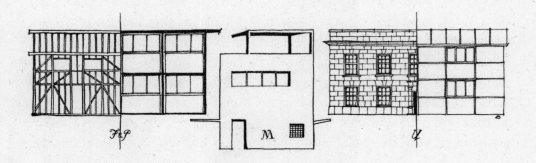

1. *Unit construction*

2. *Monolithic construction*

3. *Frame construction—reinforced concrete. The two buildings epitomise the architectural revolution.*

4. *Frame construction—wood*

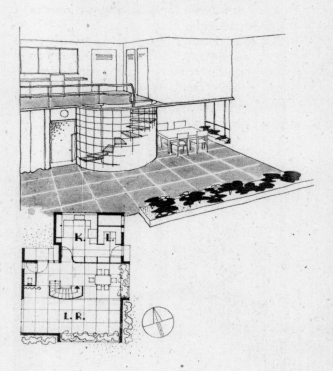

One need hardly add that other influences tended in the same direction. The break-down of economic and sex distinctions consigned the Morning Room, the Drawing Room, the Library, the Boudoir, the Smoking Room, the Billiard Room, etc., to obsolescence, and substituted for them all the spacious, informal, free-and-easy Living Room. The house could cease to be an intricate box full of small compartments and become an airy space as definitely or as indefinitely bounded as a clearing in a wood. Needless to say, architects, with their innate tendency to go in off the deep end, had no sooner realized their freedom than they abused it. Just as the garden flowed indoors, so within everything flowed into everything else. There was a violent hacking down of partitions until the " Living Space " flowed into the " Dining Space ", the " Dining Space " flowed into the " Cooking Space ", and the man with the meat flowed through the Living Room on his way to the larder. It was momentarily forgotten that all this space depended on central heating and that even with it the human spirit feels less expansive in January than in July.

But with all its absurdities (and they were less extreme here than elsewhere) the " free planning " that came in with the 'thirties had a completely healthy influence on our homes. Quite literally it swept the cobwebs away. Not only was there a tremendous horizontal liberation of space. Architects re-learnt to think in three dimensions, and the vertical section through a house became as interesting as its plan. Living rooms, like the medieval hall, might be given the full height of the house, with galleried bedrooms and an airy spiral stair twirling down therefrom. Bathrooms, once frigidly lofty, were cut right down and neatly fitted into interstices between floors. Bedrooms ran gaily out into terraces and loggias. Houses which for so long had announced to passers-by " I am correct," now called out " I am happy ". Best of all, it became possible to give a sense of space to even the narrowest-fronted city dwelling and to squeeze every inch of value out of the most restricted site.

There was nothing in the bone-structure of the monolithic house to prevent its following suit, which it proceeded to do. In practice there has been little to choose in spaciousness between the two structural types, but the framed house, standing on " pins ", generally achieved an airiness which the monolithic house, standing on "slabs", could not quite emulate. Meanwhile, as is always the case, the traditional house could not ignore the set of the tide, and there were few neo-Georgian architects who did not unbend to the extent of introducing here and there a wide steel or concrete beam, sufficient to provide a generous interior, a wide south window or a discreet loggia.

It was nothing less than an architectural revolution. The house, which through the centuries had risen quietly and heavily from its native earth, now rested quite lightly on the landscape like a great white bird.

1. " I am correct "

2. " I am happy "

3. Bungalow on the edge of the Chilterns. The window is no longer a hole in the wall. The recessed plinth gives lightness of poise.

4. Houses round a green at Frognal, Hampstead; an example of speculative building designed by an architect.

1693

2

1

3

1815

1760

THE ENGLISH

1860

4

1825

TRADITION

5

6

1890

In physiognomy certain lines and masses make a smiling face, others a frowning one. Similarly in architecture certain lines and masses make . . . one nameless effect (for language fails here), and others another. The effect X and the effect Y, though nameless and inexpressible in words, are just as definite and emotionally perceptible by the sensitive man as a smile or a frown. These effects are what architecture is made of ; and the better an architect's discrimination among them the better architect he will be.

H. S. GOODHART-RENDEL

CLOTHING

THE SKELETON thus poised upon the ground must next be clothed, and the purpose of this clothing, like any other, is partly protective, partly decorative. More accurately, the function of the walls and roof of a building is first to keep out the wet, the cold and the heat, and secondly to present a respectable and if possible beautiful appearance. And since these functions have to be discharged for the whole life of the building, it is essential that the material chosen, apart from mere durability, should either weather pleasantly or wash down easily.

There are two ways of solving this problem. The first and most obvious is to make the actual structural components do duty as covering materials. Flat roofs, bricks, stone and concrete are materials which, if well chosen, are quite capable of a double role, and where houses are built by either the " unit " or the " monolithic " methods (as described in the last chapter) one would expect this to be the solution. Where on the other hand the method is " frame and panel ", clothing must of necessity be separate from structure and we find sloping roofs, wooden boards, lath-and-plaster, glass, tiles and a host of composite sheeting materials tried in different times and places.

Machines for Living in

All this may seem excessively obvious, and in fact for centuries builders never had to give a thought to these first principles. Traditional methods and certain simple rules of thumb took care of the whole matter. But by the twentieth century the traditional ways of dressing-up a building had become stale ; every possible way had been disinterred and reinterred ; and architects were sick to death of them all. At the same moment (it was round about the first World War) they began to be aware both of the new structural possibilities already referred to and of the clean, slick beauty of machines like locomotives and steamships. Objects like the Albert Memorial came to be considered ugly, while objects like the Mauretania came to be

White walls and dark trees : the modern architect's dream

considered beautiful. People began to spell Machine with a capital M, and in face of a great deal of evidence to the contrary it was solemnly believed that if a thing does its job efficiently it will be beautiful. While this was less pernicious than the Victorian view that a useful object must be written off as ugly, it was equally mistaken.

It is easy to guess the effect of these ideas on the looks of buildings. Ornament was banished (the word ceased to be used unless qualified by the epithet "superfluous"), and with it went the various projections, copings, cornices, string courses, etc., which had traditionally served to throw rainwater clear of the wall face and protect it from penetration. Houses, like their occupants, flaunted their anatomy, and while some had beautiful bodies that (while they remained young) delighted the passer-by, others had not. Any kind of clothing for the bare concrete seemed dishonest. Pure white was *de rigueur*, partly because of its exciting novelty, partly because it emphasised the

" Faded like a flower in the frost "

smoothly mechanical texture, and pointed the contrast between it and surrounding nature. Thus with the advent of modern science the wall and roof, which for centuries had done their jobs unobtrusively, ceased effectively to bar heat and cold, sometimes ceased to be water-proof, and presented a surface which could neither be cleaned nor happily left to weather. The modern house arrived in a blaze of glory and after a brief summer of astonishing beauty faded like a flower in the frost.

Luckily, these facts had become obvious before the 'thirties ended and steps were being taken to meet them. Concrete paints and stuccos were devised to resist cracking and streakiness. Washable glazed wall-tiling of various sorts was successfully tried in London and other big towns. Above all, the advantage of materials such as brick and stone which become steadily more beautiful with age

were re-discovered. A fair number of completely modern houses were faced with brick, and it became a fashionable contrast to place walls of the roughest rubble alongside the new smooth white ones. Even the flat roof ceased to be compulsory. Eaves were allowed to project again and the great windows and walls of glass which had given the early houses so frigid an air received the protection of deep overhangs, calculated to intercept the noon summer sunlight, but allow the low sun of winter to reach wide and deep into the house. While few architects of the *avant-garde* had when the 'thirties ended yet been bold enough to use the traditional double-pitched roof, there was quite a craze for the one-pitch roof or lean-to, which was considered to avoid (to quote one of them) any " undesirable association with false romanticism ".

1

The effect of these modifications was entirely good. The boxiness of the early experiments disappeared, and with a friendlier texture came a greatly increased plasticity. The modern house which started life, as adolescents must, by fighting its environment, seemed, as the decade ended, to be coming to terms with it.

It should perhaps be mentioned here (it applies throughout this book) that all this action and reaction only went on among a small minority of architects. It was Eddington who wrote that " while an explorer is jealous of his reputation for proper caution, he cannot aspire to the quintessence of caution displayed by the man who entrenches himself at home." The great majority, entrenched among methods that made no demands on courage or imagination, sat back and watched the whole process with amusement, asking what was gained by it all.

The answer could be another quotation— say from John Stuart Mill ; " Improvement in human affairs is wholly the work of uncontented characters."

With all their crudities these houses were a new visual experience. They excited contempt and admiration, but above all they were exciting. In fact, they saved English architecture from dying of boredom.

THE RETURN TO
A FRIENDLIER TEXTURE

1. A London house showing brick used with characteristic modern precision. (But the vast spans at first-floor level are out of scale, giving the house a clown's face.)

2. (Opposite) Washable glazed tiles in London. The concrete is painted white, the side walls are of yellow London bricks.

1

2

3. The modern house dressed for the English climate. On this sort of blank grey day white walls go dirty, while warm brick and sheltering eaves seem necessary to our comfort.

THE RETURN
TO A FRIENDLIER TEXTURE

1. A row of cottages at Stratford-on-Avon, with brick front, stone sides and a lean-to roof. (The shared lawn is architecturally effective but may not be popular.)

2. Rough stone and white bricks on the Sussex coast. (The stone here compelled to leap spaces for which it was hardly designed by nature.)

Fred

TWO FACES *and a critical comparison of their features*

HERE, in parenthesis, are two houses, roughly the same size, roughly the same plan—little central lobby and staircase (one imagines), landing above it, sitting rooms to right and left below, bedrooms to right and left above. Neither is exceptionally good or exceptionally bad. Let us christen them Fred and Clarence and compare notes on them.

First note that Clarence goes to great pains to disguise the symmetry of its plan. Both bedrooms are the same size and have the same sized windows, yet one is strongly emphasized with a flamboyant surprised-looking gable and the other pushed back into the roof. Why? The only result is to break the elevation up vertically and make it impossible for the house to lie down quietly on the ground. Compare Fred's candid treatment of these windows, and hence a breadth and generosity in its plain face. The rooms are roughly the same height yet Fred lies long and low, at home in the landscape, while Clarence sits primly upright, a self-conscious foreigner. Fred's low out-

Clarence

house links it with neighbours and repeating the house's shape in miniature gives the house itself added importance. Note especially the roofing problem. Clarence makes specially heavy weather of it, yet can invent no more interesting pitch for the gables than the banal 45 degrees. Fred with a few sheets of asbestos makes it all look easy. Clarence's spindly chimney gets no support from the roof. Fred's utility version, with its capping repeating the roof slope, sits safely on the ridge. Front doors. Clarence's

hostile, high-waisted, is particularly ill-at-ease alongside the lavatory window. Fred's is carefully dressed in uniform.

I do not claim perfection for Fred. Its brickwork is of poor quality, its setting, with the thoughtless garden gate, is shabby, and its front door might have been allowed a touch of *panache*. But Fred's face is friendly, while Clarence eyes the world with the suspicion born of self-distrust.

The reality of the building does not consist of walls and roof but of the space within to be lived in.

LAO TZE

DOWNSTAIRS

LET US NOW open the front door, noticing how charming and personal a feature of the house it can be, and how much the opposite, and go inside. We are confronted by a miserable little space which you would hardly recognise as the direct descendant of the great medieval hall, (in fact, it should be given another name, for which " Lobby ", with its suggestions of Hubby and Hobby, seems the inevitable candidate). It is bound to be a small space, because unless we are very rich we cannot afford many non-habitable cubic feet. But it is worth noting how that Lilliput feeling can be exorcised by clever handling of its simple components, doors, stairs and daylight. From the " lobby "access must exist to pram-space, cloakroom, lavatory and kitchen, all of which involves some pretty little problems where the architect's ingenuity counts for everything ; and lastly to the living room, which we now enter.

We should at once be overwhelmed by sensations of spaciousness, of comfort, of sunlight (if available) and of garden beyond. We have seen in previous chapters how modern technique has made this structurally possible, and how modern life, by substituting a single living room for a suite of apartments has enabled the architect to lump all his space together instead of distributing it in small packets about the house. Notice how the word " space " recurs. Architecture is the manipulation of space. It can be squeezed, strung out, stopped, released and recaptured—so that our progress through a building is an adventure in space, just as a symphony is an adventure in sound. In this instance, we should emerge into the living room with the same sense of release as when we pass from a porch into a cathedral nave. But with this difference, that cosiness is not demanded of cathedrals. It may be easy on halcyon days with bluebottles zooming in and out, to forget the oily drizzle or the steely wind through which a man fights back towards his home, his mind full of what Freudians may call nostalgia for the womb, but which he identifies with crumpets and carpet slippers. But to ignore either mood is fatal, and it is this polarity between spaciousness and cosiness which makes the making of a lovely living room so teasing a problem.

1936

As you would expect, the modern designers of the 'thirties found it easier to achieve the spaciousness than the cosiness. Enforced economy, an almost pathological revulsion from ornament, together with a genuine feeling for air and sun, determined that of the two extreme solutions—a large room with a lot in it or a small room with nothing in it—the second should prevail. (Unfortunately there was more chance of success with the first, as the reader will discover for himself by experiment.) So we find first of all a phase of pure elimination, with white walls, simple rectangular shapes and low ceilings. Then, to relieve the austerity, an experiment with the horizontal, for which there was obvious justification. "Traditional" construction, as we have seen, dictated narrow openings; the newer methods facilitated wide ones. There was an exciting novelty in the long band of window, the long low fireplace often carried on by bookshelves the same height on which a piece of sculpture or a cactus (normally the only ornament in

1946

The post war reaction from austerity.

the room) might suitably stand. The designer sought subconsciously in the earthbound horizontal some relief from the chilly spaces he had called into being. Furniture followed suit : nothing to be over two feet high if possible, and the arms of sofas and chairs, which threatened some vertical emphasis, to be appropriately flattened out.

It was a mannerism, and therefore it died. Anyway it was not enough. As the 'thirties advanced, English designers felt their way towards the other solution—

towards a larger room with a richer texture. The ceiling was pushed up, at any rate over part of the room. The room shape became more complicated and interesting. Plants from the garden were brought in. Pictures were tolerated. Scrubbed boards and rough-hewn stone appeared, and large blazing fires were kindled in a brave attempt to loosen things up. Finally a few objects that were not strictly contemporary were quietly admitted into the room.

1. *A modern room in the grand manner. Walls of wood veneers, marble and printed fabrics. A great advance from the white period, but the gleaming surfaces and precise detailing still dictate too cruelly how you shall live.*

2. *A modernistic interior of the same period, self-consciously chromium-plated. Notice the meaningless curves, the skimpy window, the comfortless verticality of the electric fire, and the irritating black dots on the wall.*

3. Dark brown tiled floor, walls of sandblasted pine boards, chimneypiece of white concrete cast in shuttering of the same timber and furniture of rough-hewn pine and cowskin. An eccentric and brilliant example of the reaction from mechanism of the late thirties, demonstrating that nothing is more formal than studied informality. The room is a declaration of independence rather than a receptacle of ordinary life.

Meanwhile, quite different avenues were explored. Admirers of Mr. Osbert Lancaster's drawings will not need to be reminded of the wilder plunges of fashion —and anyhow this is no place for a catalogue of decorators' whimsies. But it is worth noting that they all share one fallacy, namely the assumption that beauty attends upon some horribly discreet Harmony of Style, whereas in fact it is far more likely to ignore the rules and come (as it were) down the chimney. What gives a room style is in fact not the superior knowledge of the decorator, but the peculiar habits and possessions of the owner. The decorator has always been a governess. His rooms compel you to sit and move in a certain way, to put your books or your glass here, but NOT here, to clear away old newspapers and keep a plant somehow alive in the empty corner. But the house is a machine for *living* in. If one may address one word to the decorator and to his client, it is to the former " Modesty ", and to the latter " Courage ".

After this longish meditation in the living room we pass via the dining space into the kitchen. How this transit is managed depends on the way of life of the family. If it employs a cook, the dining space is likely to be a cheerful, low-ceilinged, well-lit annex of the living room, divided or divisiblethere from by the arrangement of the furniture, and connected in its turn with the kitchen by a neatly detailed sideboard-hatch. Where the housewife cooks herself, she will generally prefer to feed her family (and park her children) in a corner of the kitchen which must be specially designed for the purpose. As for the kitchen itself, if the housewife does not get herself a well-planned kitchen, it will not be for lack of advice on how to do so. The modern kitchen is rapidly becoming as standardised and well-advertised a piece of mechanism as the family car, and in doing so has ceased to be a problem for the architect, who need only ensure that it is well lit and neatly articulated with the rest of the plan.

" You may prefer to live entirely in the air."
A nicely proportioned example of the "house on
pins."

"Have nothing in your house that you do not know to be useful or believe to be beautiful."

WILLIAM MORRIS

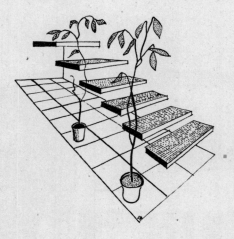

UPSTAIRS

THE TIME HAS COME to go upstairs, assuming that is, that the bedrooms, etc., *are* upstairs. Circumstances of site may put them below your living room, and the garage above it ; or you may prefer to live entirely on the ground, or entirely in the air. The modern architect greets all such variations with enthusiasm, as they force him to abandon stock solutions and give him a good chance of doing something original. There is a great deal to be said, if you have space for it, for a single storey small house, which always looks and feels more generous and more secure than our old friend the three-bedroom box. But this house we are exploring is an average one, and we go upstairs to bed.

An elegant essay in elimination. The dénouement of the staircase really seems final; one cannot believe that it will ever be dressed up again.

" The whole point of a staircase : its airy spring into space."

2

Notice the stairs. Until recently (except for an ancient legend that architects sometimes forget to put them in) nobody ever did. They had become so fussy and overdecorated that the eye habitually avoided them, and it was not till all the ornament was peeled off them that it became possible once again to take pleasure in what is after all the whole point of staircase—its airy spring into space. And this is, by the by, the great merit of our twentieth-century aversion from " applied " ornament—that we are enabled to see the thing *as a whole.* The staircase, from being a mere vehicle for elaborate decoration, becomes itself a decorative object. Lightness, here, is all ; helped by the slim grace of steel and the papery delicacy of reinforced concrete. Even with traditional wood, it seems logical enough to omit the vertical parts of steps (known as " risers ") and so facilitate cleaning and eliminate that dark and grubby little hole under the stairs. But a fashion which came in with the early 'thirties for displaying the whole staircase to the outer world through an enormous window, having no practical justification, foundered on the rocks of British commonsense.

And so to the bedrooms, which, curiously enough, have been least affected by the architectural revolution. A Georgian would be shocked by our living rooms and mystified by our kitchens and bathrooms, but he would suffer no more than a mild claustrophobia on entering a modern bedroom. Change here may have been delayed by a certain indecision about what in fact we want a bedroom to be. Space-economy and the building-in of furniture have made it smaller than it was, but its secondary use as a private sitting room has prevented our reducing it to what it otherwise might well have become — an air-conditioned sleeping-cupboard like a ship's cabin. On the whole the pre-war bedroom was uninteresting. Seldom indeed did the architect consider the view from the bed and so place and shield his windows that, without glare, one's waking view was of branches tossing in the wind or of blossom shining in the morning sun.

A London penthouse.

By way of compensation for the reduced size of the bedroom modern construction made it much easier than it had been to throw open its windows to terraces and roof gardens. The pleasures of roof gardens can be exaggerated, so long as town atmospheres remain sooty ; nor does our English dew encourage sleeping-out. Still it does seem strange that houses with enormous gardens were often given wide roof terraces that were never used, whereas the surbuban house on its tiny plot was nearly always denied this free and easy addition to its open spaces.

One of the minor problems of the flat-roofed house is the disposal of water-tanks. Where the flat roof was designed for use, a simple and effective solution was to combine the tank-room with a sun-bathing space and a secluded workroom for the owner in a little pent-house remote from the world.

A country penthouse.

SERVICES

Behind it all meanwhile unseen and ignored run the nerves and arteries of the house. More revolutionary than any development in structure is this tangle of pipes and wires that ties our modern house to the earth and links it with its neighbours. It is this invisible web that has transformed it from a mere shelter into a machine ; and it is in this aspect of building that we are likely soon to see the greatest technical innovation.

So far, the services you would expect to find laid on to your house would be cold water, with means of getting rid of it, electricity, telephone and, perhaps, gas. There are two obvious gaps in these arrangements, first heat : water has to be heated and the house warmed either by the physical effort of its owner or by extravagant small-scale use of gas or electricity. Second, refuse : the dustbin is a curious and repulsive anachronism. These gaps are on the way to being filled, probably like this. Heat and hot water will, for a transition period, be brought to the town house in pipes from central boiler houses. Ultimately atomic energy will probably reduce the cost of electricity to a point at which it becomes economic for all heating and lighting purposes. Refuse will disappear down the kitchen sink waste and be carried thence to a central incinerator whose heat will be used for some useful purpose.

Heating a house is useless unless its skin keeps the heat in. The weak points are the window cracks and their glass. Weather-stripping, as it is called, can be devised to cover the cracks, and cellular glass incorporating an airspace for insulation is on the way. Given fully effective insulation, the heat of our bodies alone (as many an ENSA show has demonstrated) suffices to warm our buildings. Without it, one is as effectively protected as a naked man drinking whisky in the snow.

Sound insulation matters too. If we are really to return to terrace building it can only be on the basis of an absolutely sound-proof party wall, and little things like the outward-opening window that reflects the radio into the adjoining living-room will need watching. Sound insulation is largely a matter of planning, whereas heat-insulation is a question of economics.

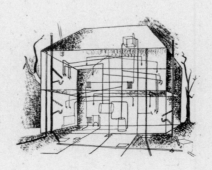

There is nothing more interesting or more important in this world today than trying to put into the houses in which our typical best citizens live something of the quality of a genuine work of art.

FRANK LLOYD WRIGHT

PROSPECTS

ARCHITECTS, as we have seen, may be divided into pioneers and general practitioners, both of them indispensable. We have now surveyed in some detail the struggles of the pioneers and it is time to decide what it all amounts to in terms of the general practice of today. Let us sum up the net gain under four headings.

1. *Setting.*

Houses became more neighbourly, grouped in terraces or around greens. The individual house opened itself to the sun and established a friendly relationship with trees and plants.

2. *Structure.*

New ways of building suggested " free " planning. The house was conceived from the inside outwards and aspect and orientation took precedence over symmetry. The structure seemed to be poised lightly on the earth.

3. *Outsides.*

The house was deliberately made to contrast with surrounding nature instead of trying to harmonize with it. A much greater variety of facing material was accepted, notably glass and wood. Roofs could be flat, single-pitch or double-pitch, and the house silhouette could vary accordingly.

4. *Insides.*

The loosely flowing plan involved a great liberation of space. The big informal living room became the dominating feature of the house, while kitchen and bathroom became highly mechanised and of minimum size. Terraces and roof-gardens linked indoors and outdoors.

Obviously your post-war house is going to reflect these tendencies—does so already, where it exists. Let us look at some of the best of the " permanent prefabs " (officially and absurdly referred

1-4. Four of the permanent " prefabs " showing the influence of the experiments of the thirties on the working-class house. The order of merit should be obvious.

to as "non-traditional" houses to distinguish them from the temporaries) and see which way the wind blows. Most of them are frame-and-panel houses, the frames being of steel or reinforced concrete and the panels of steel sheets, precast concrete, lath and plaster or some sort of structural sandwich. Most of them are built "dry" (like a barn) rather than "wet" (like a mud-hut), and they are called prefabs because the frame and panels, as well as the equipment, are ready-made and mass-produced instead of being made to measure. As for their looks, some are handsome, others ugly. The problem generally has been to breathe grace and humanity into the rigidly rectangular three-dimensional grid that is their skeleton. Where, by intense struggle that looks like the wave of a magic wand, this has been done, the result is architecture. Where the grim little box with its square holes and panels resembles a child's patent constructional toy, it is just building, and only the merciful hand of the town-planner and his partner Nature can redeem it. The man who buys a mass-produced car is reminded of his human dignity by the fact that he can choose its colour. Similarly most makers of these homes have rightly given the buyer a choice of interior plans and external porches. And one negative merit they all have : they appear to be what they are. It is too soon to say that we have seen the last of the "Tudorbethan", but these houses, light, bright, plain and clean, perched delicately upon the squalid morasses of our post-war housing sites, are at least solid proof that

3

4

the work of the pioneers can quite soon become general practice.

The years ahead of us are not going to bring startling novelties. Those marginal items which turn a decent building into a distinguished one are likely to be firmly blue-pencilled by the licensing authorities —a situation well worth enduring if it helps to build up, on the foundations laid in the 'thirties, a sound and simple vernacular. The huge number of houses needed will in itself impose a unity on our new streets and our individualism can be trusted to see that it doesn't degenerate to uniformity. We shall be forced to pre-fabricate both our houses and their components. Walls, floors, roofs, windows, kitchens, bathrooms, piping will arrive complete, and the builder's job will be one of assembly rather than construction. The same urgency will encourage the use of dry sheeting materials and the avoidance of plasters and paints which take time to dry out. Lastly, the necessity of keeping the town reasonably compact will force us to group our houses, and blitz experience will create a demand for those shared amenities, from district heating to day nurseries, which transform a mere estate into a community.

Nothing sensational, but the wide and steady infiltration of decent standards—that is the best we can hope for. And the danger—not immediate but not remote—a wild and woolly reaction from Utility which could liquidate the new standards before they have set and turn the Great Exhibition of 195? into the atomic equivalent of its notorious predecessor.

And meanwhile, a new generation of pioneers prepares to make itself unpopular. It will be its task to satisfy the demand for rococo pleasures and baroque thrills which is bound to come. It must tackle the subleties of the monumental and the problems of ornament. In its hands the cactus must learn to flower.

In my end is my beginning

INDEX OF ILLUSTRATIONS

*Photographs are the copyright of the author, except where
another name is given in brackets*

*Printed for Penguin Books Ltd by Harrison & Sons Ltd, Printers to His Majesty the King,
London, Hayes (Middx) and High Wycombe*

64